D1709585

My First Animal Library

Giraffes

by Rebecca Stromstad Glaser

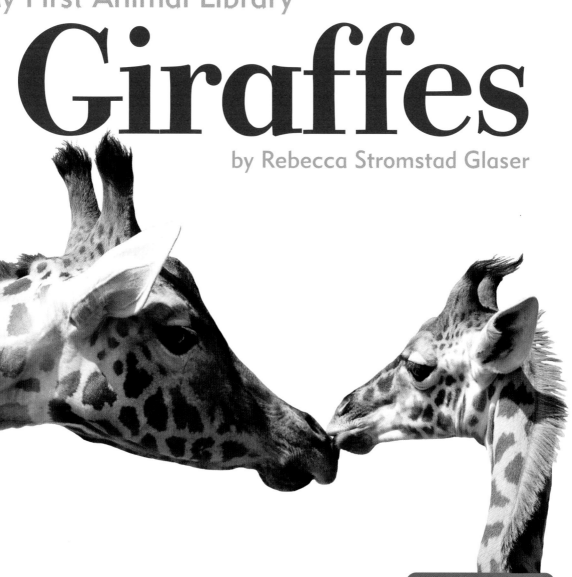

Bullfrog Books

Ideas for Parents and Teachers

Bullfrog Books give children practice reading nonfiction at the earliest levels. Repetition, familiar words, and photos support early readers.

Before Reading
- Discuss the cover photo. What does it tell them?
- Look at the picture glossary together. Read and discuss the words.

Read the Book
- "Walk" through the book and look at the photos. Let the child ask questions. Point out the photo labels.
- Read the book to the child, or have him or her read independently.

After Reading
- Prompt the child to think more. Ask: What is your favorite part of a giraffe? Why? How do giraffes avoid their enemies?

Bullfrog Books are published by Jump!
5357 Penn Avenue South
Minneapolis, MN 55419
www.jumplibrary.com

Library of Congress Cataloging-in-Publication Data
Glaser, Rebecca Stromstad.
 Giraffes / by Rebecca Stromstad Glaser.
  p. cm. — (Bullfrog books. My first animal library, zoo animals)
 Summary: "This easy-to-read nonfiction book tells how tall giraffes are, how their unique body features help them adapt to their habitat, and how they survive" — Provided by publisher.
 Audience: 005.
 Audience: K to grade 3.
 Includes bibliographical references and index.
 ISBN 978-1-62031-063-2 (hardcover)
 ISBN 978-1-62496-064-2 (ebook)
 1. Giraffe —Juvenile literature. I. Title.
 QL737.U56G58 2014
 599.638--dc23
                                        2013008543

Editors Wendy Dieker and Quinn Arnold
Series Designer Ellen Huber
Book Designer Lindaanne Donohoe
Book Production Sean Melom

Photo Credits: All photos Shutterstock except iStockPhoto, 8–9; National Geographic, 19; Alamy. 20–21

Printed in the United States at Corporate Graphics in North Mankato, Minnesota.
5-2013 / PO 1003
10 9 8 7 6 5 4 3 2 1

Table of Contents

The Tallest Animal

What is the tallest
animal in the world?

A giraffe!

Males are the tallest.

They can look in an upstairs window.

calf

A baby giraffe is tall, too.
A newborn calf is as tall
as a man.

A giraffe has a long neck.

It is the longest of any animal.

It can reach the treetops.

A giraffe has a long tongue.

acacia
leaves

It grabs leaves
from an acacia
tree. Yum!

13

It's time for a drink.

A giraffe spreads out its legs.

Now it can reach the water.

One giraffe watches.
She can see enemies
far away.

hyena

Oh no! A lion!

All the giraffes run.
Now they are safe.

Time to rest.

They sleep standing up.

Good night, giraffes!

Parts of a Giraffe

horn
Males use their horns
when they fight.

spots
A giraffe's spots help it blend
in with its surroundings and
hide from enemies.

neck
Giraffes have the
longest neck of any
animal.

tail
Giraffes use their
tails to keep
insects away.

22

Picture Glossary

acacia tree
A tree with feathery leaves that grows in Africa.

enemy
An animal that could hurt a giraffe.

calf
A young giraffe.

male
A boy giraffe.

Index

To Learn More

Learning more is as easy as 1, 2, 3.

1) Go to www.factsurfer.com

2) Enter "giraffes" into the search box.

3) Click the "Surf" button to see a list of websites.

With factsurfer.com, finding more information is just a click away.